TRIANGLE HISTORIES
★★★★★ ★★★★★
THE REVOLUTIONARY WAR

THOMAS PAINE

Kate Davis

BLACKBIRCH®
PRESS

THOMSON
———★———
™
GALE

San Diego • Detroit • New York • San Francisco • Cleveland
New Haven, Conn. • Waterville, Maine • London • Munich

For more information, contact
The Gale Group, Inc.
27500 Drake Rd.
Farmington Hills, MI 48331-3535
Or you can visit our Internet site at http://www.gale.com

Photo credits: Cover, cover (inset), pages 5, 7, 36, 41, 50, 65, 70, 78 © North Wind Picture Archives; pages 9, 18, 19, 21, 35, 75, 81 © Bettman/CORBIS; page 10 © Gianni Dagli Orti/CORBIS; pages 13, 72 © Historical Picture Archive/CORBIS; page 30, 32, 39, 57, 60, 67, 85, 95 © historypictures.com; pages 27, 43, 55, 58, 88, 93 © Archiving Early America.

LIBRARY OF CONGRESS CATALOGING-IN-PUBLICATION DATA

Davis, Kate, 1951-
  Thomas Paine / by Kate Davis.
    p. cm. — (Triangle history of the American Revolution. Revolutionary War leaders)
  Summary: A biography of Thomas Paine, who spent his youth in England but became a hero of the American and French revolutions by writing books and pamphlets which embodied the ideals of freedom, equality, and democracy.
  Includes bibliographical references and index.
  ISBN 1-56711-611-6
  1. Paine, Thomas, 1737-1809. 2. Political scientists-United States—Biography. 3. Revolutionaries—United States—Biography. [1. Paine, Thomas, 1737-1809. 2. Political scientists. 3. Revolutionaries.] I. Title. II. Series.
  JC178.V5 D38 2003
  320.51′092—dc21
                                                                 2002010704

Printed in China
10 9 8 7 6 5 4 3 2 1

CONTENTS

PREFACE: THE AMERICAN REVOLUTION

Today, more than two centuries after the final shots were fired, the American Revolution remains an inspiring story not only to Americans, but also to people around the world. For many citizens, the well-known battles that occurred between 1775 and 1781—such as Lexington, Trenton, Yorktown, and others—represent the essence of the Revolution. In truth, however, the formation of the United States involved much more than the battles of the Revolutionary War. The creation of our nation occurred over several decades, beginning in 1763, at the end of the French and Indian War, and continuing until 1790, when the last of the original 13 colonies ratified the Constitution.

More than 200 years later, it may be difficult to fully appreciate the courage and determination of the people who fought for, and founded, our nation. The decision to declare independence was not made easily—and it was not unanimous. Breaking away from England—the ancestral land of most colonists—was a bold and difficult move. In addition to the emotional hardship of revolt, colonists faced the greatest military and economic power in the world at the time.

The first step on the path to the Revolution was essentially a dispute over money. By 1763, England's treasury had been drained in order to pay for the French and Indian War. British lawmakers, as well as England's new ruler, King George III, felt that the colonies should help to pay for the war's expense and for the cost of housing the British troops who remained in the colonies. Thus began a series of oppressive British tax acts and other laws that angered the colonists and eventually provoked full-scale violence.

King George III

The Stamp Act of 1765 was followed by the Townshend
Acts in 1767. Gradually, colonists were forced to pay
taxes on dozens of everyday goods from playing cards to
paint to tea. At the same time, the colonists had no say in
the passage of these acts. The more colonists complained
that "taxation without representation is tyranny," the
more British lawmakers claimed the right to make laws

for the colonists "in all cases whatsoever." Soldiers and tax collectors were sent to the colonies to enforce the new laws. In addition, the colonists were forbidden to trade with any country but England.

Each act of Parliament pushed the colonies closer to unifying in opposition to English laws. Boycotts of British goods inspired protests and violence against tax collectors. Merchants who continued to trade with the Crown risked attacks by their colonial neighbors. The rising violence soon led to riots against British troops stationed in the colonies and the organized destruction of British goods. Tossing tea into Boston Harbor was just one destructive act. That event, the Boston Tea Party, led England to pass the so-called Intolerable Acts of 1774. The port of Boston was closed, more British troops were sent to the colonies, and many more legal rights for colonists were suspended.

Finally, there was no turning back. Early on an April morning in 1775, at Lexington Green in Massachusetts, the first shots of the American Revolution were fired. Even after the first battle, the idea of a war against England seemed unimaginable to all but a few radicals. Many colonists held out hope that a compromise could be reached. Except for the Battle of Bunker Hill and some minor battles at sea, the war ceased for much of 1775. During this time, delegates to the Continental Congress struggled to reach a consensus about the next step.

During those uncertain months, the Revolution was fought, not on a military battlefield, but on the battlefield of public opinion. Ardent rebels—especially Samuel Adams and Thomas Paine—worked tirelessly to keep the spirit of revolution alive. They stoked the fires of revolt by writing letters and pamphlets, speaking at public gatherings, organizing boycotts, and devising other forms of protest. It was their brave efforts that kept others focused on liberty and freedom until July 4, 1776. On that day, Thomas Jefferson's Declaration of Independence left no doubt about the intentions of the colonies. As John Adams wrote afterward, the "revolution began in hearts and minds not on the battlefield."

As unifying as Jefferson's words were, the United States did not become a nation the moment the Declaration of Independence claimed the right of all people to "life, liberty, and the pursuit of happiness." Before, during, and after the war, Americans who spoke of their "country" still generally meant whatever colony was their home. Some colonies even had their own navies during the war, and a few sent their own representatives to Europe to seek aid for their colony alone while delegates from the Continental Congress were doing the same job for the whole United States. Real national unity did not begin to take hold until the inauguration of George Washington in 1789, and did not fully bloom until the dawn of the 19th century.

The story of the American Revolution has been told for more than two centuries and may well be told for centuries to come. It is a tribute to the men and women who came together during this unique era that, to this day, people the world over find inspiration in the story of the Revolution. In the words of the Declaration of Independence, these great Americans risked "their lives, their fortunes, and their sacred honor" for freedom.

The Minuteman statue stands in Concord, Massachusetts.

Introduction:
"A Cause for
All Mankind"

Tall, broad-shouldered Thomas Paine leaned into the wind in February 1776. A gust ruffled the papers he held as he walked down the streets of colonial Philadelphia.

Four weeks had passed since printer Robert Bell had published a pamphlet Paine had written, called *Common Sense*. Bell had summoned Paine to the print shop that morning. The timing was good, because Paine had recently revised some of the writing.

Common Sense was the best piece he had ever written, Paine believed. In it, he insisted that the American colonies should sever ties with England completely. Some colonists felt Paine was a genius for his clear reasoning about the necessity of revolution. Others wanted him hanged for treason.

Common Sense stated that war was necessary if independence were to be won. The British army had fired on Patriots at Lexington, near Boston, Massachusetts, almost a year earlier. A revolution at this point, Paine believed, was a battle for all colonists.

Despite his zeal for a revolution, Paine had come to America only a little more than a year earlier. He had signed *Common Sense* "Written by an Englishman." By February 1776, word had spread that Paine was the author.

When Paine reached Bell's shop, he learned that the first printing of *Common Sense* had sold out. The profit was 30 pounds, to be divided between Bell and Paine. As much as he needed the money, Paine asked that his earnings be sent to the Patriot army.

Thomas Paine is credited with writing the words that most inspired the colonists to fight for independence.

No sooner had Bell explained the rapid sales of *Common Sense* than the shop door opened and an elderly gentlemen stepped in. It was Benjamin Franklin, whom Paine had not seen in several weeks.

After the two men exchanged greetings, Franklin complimented Paine on his pamphlet, which Franklin had reviewed when it was in an early draft.

Paine asked Franklin about the effect of his writing on the Continental Congress, which was then meeting in nearby Carpenter's Hall to decide what steps the colonies would take. The delegates remained divided, Franklin said. Massachusetts delegate Samuel Adams considered *Common Sense* a brilliant piece of propaganda. Those who were still loyal to the Crown, though, were angered by the work. Others were caught between the two extremes. "We must act now to claim our natural rights," Paine replied. "Because it is not a cause for America alone. It is a cause for all mankind!"

9

Chapter 1

A FREETHINKER
IS FORMED

Although he came to the American colonies just a short time before the American Revolution began, Thomas Paine's contribution to the cause of freedom was one of the most significant of any Patriot in the early years of the conflict. Paine's great skill gave him notoriety as a writer whose pen could rouse the American colonists. His work was both hailed and cursed, and so was he.

OPPOSITE: Colonial London was one of the wealthiest cities in the world in the 1700s.

For most of his life, Paine struggled with poverty and loneliness. He made friends easily in working-class and political circles. Yet he lost them quickly when he made requests for support or voiced his radical thoughts. Paine was a man who could be both charming and hostile, whose political ideas helped shape the United States, and whose words shaped the thoughts of freethinking minds not only in the colonies, but everywhere.

Early Life

Thomas Paine was not originally an American, and his last name was not originally spelled with a final "e." He was born in the small town of Thetford, England, on January 29, 1737.

Thomas's mother, Frances, was 11 years older than his father, Joseph Pain. Frances was said to be "sour and eccentric," as well as temperamental. She thought of herself as Joseph's superior not only in age but in class. Her father was a well-to-do lawyer.

Joseph Pain, the son of a shoemaker, worked with his hands. Thomas described his father as a "poor but honest man." He worked as a staymaker who cut, sewed, and fitted women's corsets. His hard work paid him about 30 pounds a year.

Thomas's mother and father argued frequently, and Thomas was often caught in the middle. Not only did his parents differ in class and age, but also in religion. Frances Pain was an Anglican,

At Quaker worship services, both men and women spoke about their religious feelings.

a member of the Church of England. She and her sister saw to it that Thomas was baptized and confirmed in the Anglican Church. They taught the boy church rules and catechism. He was forced to memorize long Bible passages.

Joseph Pain was a Quaker. Quakers—members of the Society of Friends—were allowed to worship in England, but their faith was not as widely

13

accepted as the Anglican faith, which had been the official Christian religion of Great Britain since the 1500s. Because Joseph had allowed Thomas to be baptized in the Church of England, Pain was no longer permitted to attend Quaker meetings. Still, he stayed true to his faith and tried to impress his son with his beliefs in nonviolence and the existence of a divine spirit in all people.

The Pain household was frequently filled with arguments about religion and finances. The poverty and tension caused Thomas to feel that he had "all the inconveniences of early life against me."

Education

Thomas did have some advantages over other lower-middle-class children of his day. He was doted on by his parents. Thomas had enough to eat, despite his family's meager circumstances, because his parents did not have numerous mouths to feed. Frances had given birth to a daughter one year after Thomas, but the baby died in infancy.

In the mid-1700s, parents had to pay for their children to be educated, a luxury the Pains could not afford. Because Joseph was a freeman—a subject who paid a yearly tax to the town government—Thomas was allowed to attend Thetford Grammar School at the age of 7. The school was funded by a wealthy noble. Still, Thomas's parents sacrificed to pay for his school supplies.

In school, Thomas learned to read and write. He even wrote poetry, though his parents considered it impractical. When he was 8, he wrote about the death of his pet crow:

Here lies the body of John Crow
Who once was high, but now is low;
Ye brother crows take warning all,
For as you rise, so must you fall.

One subject Thomas disliked in school was Latin. For one thing, he did not like to learn languages. For another, his father felt that the use of Latin as the official language of government and the church made laws and beliefs harder for commoners to understand. Thomas's mother, on the other hand, urged him to study the language, for she knew he would need it if he went on to higher education.

Rather than read the original language, Thomas read translations of Latin books. He also studied philosophy and mathematics, both of which came easily to him. Thomas enjoyed science most of all, and said it was the "natural bent of my mind." When he read a book from his school's well-stocked library on the natural history of Virginia, he vowed to go to America one day.

Thomas dreamed of such adventure all through grammar school. Those dreams of travel were fueled by his teacher, Reverend William Knowles, who had been a chaplain on a ship in the royal navy. Knowles told stories of his travels to India, Africa, and North America.

15

Apprenticeship

When Thomas reached the age of 13, his parents could no longer afford to continue his education. Because he did not know Latin, he would never be accepted at a university. He left school and went to work as an apprentice in his father's corset shop.

To make undergarments for upper-class ladies was a tedious job. The corsets contained whalebone stays—frames—that pinched a woman's figure into the hourglass shape that was fashionable in the 18th century. During his teenage years, Thomas measured, cut, and sewed cloth, then cut, filed, and fit whalebone stays.

As he spent many hours alone with his father, Thomas learned more about the Quaker religion. Quakers believed that God dwelled in every person, and that there was no need for the structure or traditions of an established church. They took care of others in the community, sympathized with society's less fortunate, and believed in equality for all people.

★

In the early 1750s, George Washington led several military expeditions to the Ohio River Valley.

★

These freethinking beliefs threatened the official Church of England, whose leaders had rigid beliefs about the relationship between religious leaders and those who followed their faith. Although Quakers were tolerated in England in the 1750s, a Quaker could not vote, attend state universities, or hold positions in government or the military. As a result of the discrimination he experienced as a Quaker, Joseph Pain had a deep distrust of authority. During the years he worked side by side with Thomas, he conveyed his views to his son.

Restless Spirit

Although Thomas would one day say he had acquired an "exceedingly good moral education" from his father, he longed for a more exciting life. Work and prayer left little room for fun. "If the taste of a Quaker could have been consulted at the Creation," wrote Thomas, "what a silent and drab-colored Creation it would have been! Not a flower would have blossomed its gaieties, nor a bird been permitted to sing."

A market town, Thetford was home to all kinds of shops. Craftspeople, such as weavers, shoemakers, clothiers, saddlemakers, tinsmiths, carpenters, bakers, grocers, and apothecaries, were a large presence in the town. Thetford's biggest claim to fame was that the craftsmen's hall had been built by Sir Joseph Williamson, who founded England's first newspaper, the *London Gazette*.

The town had little to amuse a young man. Life for most townsfolk was constant work. Those who were not industrious sank into poverty, and some turned to robbery. In the 1700s, theft was a crime punishable by hanging in England. Thomas could see Gallows Hill, where hangings were carried out, from the window of his home.

After Thomas had worked with him for several years, Joseph Pain arranged for him to go south to

The Society of Friends

The Society of Friends, better known as the Quakers, is a religious movement that began in the mid-1600s in England. George Fox, a weaver's son, attended the Anglican Church with his parents until he was 19 years old. At that point, he became disillusioned with the strict organization and ceremonies of the faith. He spent several years traveling around England in search of a church or a religious leader that offered a religion that was closer to his inner feelings about worship.

George Fox's religious beliefs differed from those of most English Christians.

In 1647, Fox had a sudden revelation that led him to establish the Society of Friends. The group took its name from a Bible verse in which Jesus says, "I have called you friends, for all that I have heard from my Father I have made known to you." The new faith was based on Fox's belief that Jesus, the center of the Christian faith, is alive in the heart of true Christians. To Fox, this meant that there was no need for an established church, for religious leaders, or for traditional ceremonies. A "Friend" was someone who had undergone a life-changing encounter with Jesus and dedicated his or her life to this new faith.

Within a few years, Fox's religious movement had thousands of followers throughout Great Britain. There, people who opposed the new religion tried to insult its followers, and called them "Quakers" because they trembled as they spoke. The insult, though, was taken as a compliment by Fox's followers, and it became their unofficial name.

The first Quakers to arrive in the colonies came to Massachusetts in 1656. That colony was governed by rigid followers of the Puritan faith, who banished the Quakers from the colony for their beliefs. In 1681, William Penn, a wealthy member of the Friends, received a colonial land grant from King Charles II. Penn and his followers established the colony of Pennsylvania— whose name means "Penn's woods"—and founded Philadelphia, the city that became a center of the American Revolution.

Penn established the colony under a document he wrote called the *Frame of Government for Pennsylvania*. Many of the principles set forth in the document, such as religious freedom and equal rights, became the inspiration for the founders of the U.S. government a century later.

Quakers who attempted to worship in Boston in the 1650s were whipped and exiled by those who followed the Puritan faith.

London in 1756 to learn his trade under master staymaker John Morris. The city of London, with a population 300 times that of Thetford, provided Thomas with new sights and sounds—crowded streets and shops filled with exotic goods from Europe and beyond.

Although his surroundings were different, Thomas's workdays were still filled with drudgery. All through his teens, he had been bent over his workbench all day. He could not imagine a lifetime career as a staymaker. He desperately yearned for new horizons. The seafaring stories his teacher had once told began to fill his daydreams.

Close Call

Soon after Thomas began to work for Morris, he ran away. The tall 19-year-old was determined to find adventure. He thought he was skilled enough to be a valuable sail mender, so he sought work on board a privateer ship at the docks. The ship was called the *Terrible*, and it sailed under command of Captain William Death.

A privateer was a ship commissioned by the British Crown to chase enemy merchant ships and capture their cargo. Privateering was a legal, profitable business for a captain and crew, because they were allowed to keep or auction confiscated goods. Young men found work aboard a privateer an exciting way to make quick money and also to serve their country. Thomas was one who found the work attractive. He was "heated with false heroism," as he later wrote.

The time in which Thomas chose to go to sea was particularly exciting for the crews of privateers. In 1756, England was in the midst of the Seven Years' War with France, which was fought in both Europe and America, where it was known as the French and Indian War. Privateers were needed to capture supplies and not allow them to reach French forces in North America.

Sailors who served on privateers often earned more money than sailors in the British navy.

As adventurous as this work appeared, it was, like most life at sea, dangerous and uncomfortable. Crew quarters below decks were horribly over-crowded, which often led to disease. Captains could be brutal. Captured sailors might face imprisonment on foreign soil or be forced to sail for another ship under a foreign flag.

21

Joseph Pain was aware of such dangers. As soon as he heard that Thomas had plans to join Death's crew, he hurried after his son. He reached Thomas just before the *Terrible* set sail and convinced him not to go. Though neither father nor son knew it at the time, they later learned that it was fortunate Thomas had not gone. In a battle that took place a short time after the ship left port, the *Terrible* lost almost every man onboard, including Death.

A Second Attempt

Thomas Paine returned to Morris's corset shop, but not for long. In the winter of 1757, he signed on with another privateer, the *King of Prussia*. The ship had a crew of 250 men, many of nationalities other than British. This time, at age 20, Paine successfully set sail.

Like most sailors, the crew of the privateer was rugged men who spoke their minds, and felt free to criticize the captain. After all, they claimed, a captain could not sail a ship alone. A ship was only as good as the crew that sailed it, and a captain who did not treat his men fairly could end up with mutiny—a revolt—of his crew. It was during his voyage on the *King of Prussia* that Paine began to develop the idea—revolutionary for its time—that rulers ought to be answerable to their subjects or face rebellion.

When Thomas arrived back in port after the voyage, he did not sign on to another ship. He had seen his share of action on the *King of Prussia*,

22

which had overtaken a French vessel and recovered
two others seized by the enemy. He had enjoyed
the vast ocean, but months of wormy biscuits for
food and life among the rats and insects that
infested the ship made the thought of returning to
sea unbearable. He went back to London with about
30 pounds in his pocket—as much as his father
made in a whole year—and counted himself lucky.

An Independent Education

In August 1758, back in London, Paine felt a new
confidence because he had taken a risk and exercised
his independence. He bought books, globes, and
charts, and sought to learn more about astronomy
and geography. He joined other craftsmen who
wanted to improve their minds, and he attended
scientific and philosophic lectures. Afterward, in
taverns, he took part in long discussions and
debates.

Before long, the money Paine had made as a
sailor ran out, and he needed to find a means of
support. He decided to be a staymaker again, and
soon moved southeast to Dover, on the coast. After
a year, he opened a shop in nearby Sandwich. He
began to follow the teachings of a new religion
established in 1742 by a traveling preacher named
John Wesley. This branch of the Christian faith was
called Methodism, and its followers were known as
Methodists.

Unlike Quakers, Methodists believed that ministers
or preachers were necessary to direct a worship

23

service. Unlike Anglicans, Methodists believed that anyone, male or female, could become a preacher without years of rigorous training in Latin, Greek, and religious ceremony. Methodists were required to follow many of the same social commitments as Quakers. Those who wished to preach were asked to form small worship groups in their communities.

The Methodist religion attracted Paine for its social commitment as well as its rejection of strict Anglican rules for becoming a preacher. He began to preach to small groups in Sandwich, where he sometimes spoke at a meeting in a follower's home or outside. During his time in Sandwich, a young woman named Mary Lambert, who worked as a maid, caught Paine's eye. The two married in 1759, and Mary soon became pregnant. Paine's business was poor and he quickly fell deeply into debt. To avoid his creditors and to find healthier surroundings for his wife, who was ill, the Paines left Sandwich. They landed in the village of Margate. A few months later, Mary died, along with the baby, in childbirth.

★

In 1759, George Washington married Martha Custis, who was the wealthiest widow in Virginia.

★

Paine, now 23 and without a wife or a job, decided to apply to become a tax collector. He went home to Thetford to study for the exam that was given for the position. He passed and was appointed by the Board of Excise Commissioners to a post in the Midlands. Less than two years later, he was reassigned to a district southeast of London to assess and collect

Thomas Paine

taxes on alcohol, salt, soap, tobacco, and various other goods.

Men who worked as tax collectors were not popular. Merchants detested them, townspeople looked down on them, and highwaymen robbed them. In order to keep good relations with merchants, some tax collectors underestimated the true value of goods so the tax would be less. Paine sometimes stamped goods to indicate they had been taxed even if he had not really examined them. He was not a very good tax collector for King George III. In 1765, he was fired for incompetence.

For the next three years, Paine drifted around England. He tried to live with his parents again, then returned to London. He petitioned the Excise Board to reinstate him. It did, but there was no post open. He taught English briefly and found some work as a preacher. While he waited for a tax position to open, he renewed the acquaintances in the scientific and intellectual circles he had enjoyed while he worked as a staymaker.

Finally, in February 1768, he was assigned to collect excise taxes again, this time in the town of Lewes. There, he lodged with a tobacco seller named Samuel Ollive, his wife, and their daughter, Elizabeth. In Lewes, Paine worked with the church to aid the poor, and he became well liked around town. He was elected to the town council, called the Society of Twelve.

After work, Paine often met with men in the Headstrong Club at the White Hart Inn to argue

25

Benjamin Franklin

Few Americans in the 18th century were as world famous as Benjamin Franklin. His long life, from 1706 to 1790, spanned almost the entire century, and he was one of the founders of the United States.

Franklin served as a printer's apprentice under his brother in his birthplace of Boston until age 17, when he ran away to Philadelphia. By age 21, Franklin was a partner in a print shop, and by age 30, he was one of the most successful businessmen in the city. By age 42, he was able to retire due to his business success and the profits from his *Poor Richard's Almanack*, a collection of sayings and essays that he published regularly.

Franklin's fame in Europe arose in part from his writing, but he also gained renown as a result of his scientific experiments. In 1752, he flew a kite in a lightning storm to prove the connection between lightning and electricity. Franklin was awarded the Copley Medal of the Royal Society of London for this research. Among his other scientific contributions were his development of the heat-efficient Franklin stove and his drawing of the first chart of the Gulf Stream current in the Atlantic Ocean.

By the time he was in his 60s, Franklin had become a spokesman for the colonists in their anti-tax revolt against

England. He appeared
before Parliament in the
1760s to explain the
colonies' objections
to British policies.
In 1776, Franklin
went to Paris,
where, for
the duration
of the
Revolution,
he attempted
to secure
loans from
France and
other European
governments
to aid the
American cause.
In 1783, he was
among the signers
of the Treaty of Paris
that officially ended the
Revolution.

Franklin died in 1790 in
Philadelphia. His procession

Benjamin Franklin was a
famous and influential
figure in the 1700s.

through the streets of the city was accompanied by more
than 20,000 mourners. Soon after his burial, people began
to leave pennies on his tombstone in the belief that it
would bring good luck.

political issues. After each meeting, the members voted on which of the group should receive the Headstrong Book, which was awarded to the person who was most stubborn in his opinions and refused to concede that he had lost an argument. In the book, other members wrote humorous rhymes or essays that made fun of the Headstrong winner. Paine was awarded the book on many occasions during his years in the club. He also wrote a number of humorous essays, rhymes, and songs during those years for other winners.

In 1771, Paine married Elizabeth Ollive. Samuel Ollive had died in 1769, so the couple continued to live at and help Elizabeth's mother run the tobacco shop. Despite their work, the shop lost money, and Paine's salary was so low that they struggled to make ends meet.

Other excise officers suffered as well. The tax collectors banded together and asked Paine to write a formal petition to Parliament to ask for a raise in their salaries. The piece, *Case of the Officers of Excise*, was Paine's first pamphlet. In it, he described the struggles to support a family on an officer's salary and corruption in the excise business caused by officers who took bribes to supplement their pay. The other tax collectors chipped in to send Paine to London, where he presented the pamphlet to the members of Parliament.

Unfortunately for the excise officers, the petition failed. Even worse for Paine, high-ranking tax officials said he had abandoned his post without leave to go away and argue for a raise. As a result, he was stripped of his job. Paine's anger over this treatment increased when he heard rumors that George III had given himself an enormous annual increase in his expense budget.

The Paines were in such dire financial straits that their belongings were auctioned off. Elizabeth finally separated from Paine to live with her brother. At age 36, Paine was alone, homeless, and nearly penniless. He desperately needed someone to give him a hand up. That aid came in the person of Benjamin Franklin.

Chapter 2

PASSAGE TO AMERICA

Paine first met Benjamin Franklin briefly in 1768. As a lover of science, Paine was well aware of the Philadelphian who had developed such innovations as the Franklin stove and the lightning rod. Paine also admired Franklin as the writer of *Poor Richard's Almanack*, a collection of sayings and witty essays that was popular in Europe and was second only to the Bible in book sales in the colonies. Franklin was one of the most famous Americans in the world when Paine was introduced to him at a scientific lecture.

OPPOSITE: Philadelphia was one of the largest cities in the world in the 1700s.

Franklin met King George III in London in 1768.

In 1774, their paths crossed again. Paine got word that Franklin, almost 70 years old, had returned to London as a diplomat for the colonies at the English court. Paine, who had by then considered leaving England for a new life in the colonies, sought out the esteemed American. That meeting and a brief letter of introduction from Franklin changed the course of Paine's life.

Off to Philadelphia

Franklin found Paine to be a charming conversationalist. He especially admired Paine's ability to make a point in a clear and straightforward manner. He described Paine as "an ingenious worthy young man."

When Paine told Franklin that he wished to start a new life in the colonies, the American agreed to provide a recommendation for him. Franklin wrote a letter of introduction to his son-in-law in Pennsylvania and to his son, William, the royal governor of New Jersey. "I request you to give him your best advice," Franklin wrote, and asked them to help Paine find employment. Franklin was Philadelphia's most famous resident, and a recommendation from such a renowned celebrity was of great assistance.

Paine was able to borrow the money for his passage to America from some former companions in the Headstrong Club. It was a difficult voyage. Typhoid fever broke out on the ship and some passengers died. By the time the vessel reached Philadelphia, in late November 1774, Paine was so sick that he was unable to roll over in bed. The letter of introduction that attested to his friendship with Franklin secured the desperately ill Paine attention and lodging from a physician.

As soon as he recovered, Paine felt quite at home in the "city of brotherly love," founded by Quaker William Penn. In Pennsylvania, both the poor lower classes and skilled craftsmen played roles in public affairs. Although wealthy aristocrats had the greatest power in government, Paine was inspired by the possibilities of a democratic government.

After he regained his health, Paine landed a job as a tutor for friends of Franklin's son-in-law. As he had hoped, Paine had found a chance to start over. To signify his break from his former life as a debt-ridden staymaker and tax collector, he added the final letter *e* to his name.

33

On the Brink of Revolution

By early 1775, Paine's new home of Philadelphia, as well as the rest of the colonies, had edged closer to violent revolution. The unrest had begun as a result of more than a decade of unpopular British tax policies in the colonies and the British Parliament's determination to force colonists to buy English goods.

In December 1773, colonists in Boston, Massachusetts, had revolted against George III in one of the most famous incidents in American history—the Boston Tea Party. The incident came about because the British East India Company had an oversupply of tea to sell, but did not have the money to pay the import taxes in England. Parliament wanted to help the company and make money for its treasury as well. The lawmakers decided to let the company sell the tea to the colonists but did not make it pay any duty. The money would be made up by the tax the colonists paid to buy the tea. The colonists would benefit, according to British reasoning, because the cost of the tea would be lower than the tea they smuggled in illegally.

Most colonists did not see it that way at all. To have the tea forced on them was one more example of how they lacked a voice in their own affairs. In Boston, where the spirit of independence seemed strongest, colonist Samuel Adams—a failed tax collector like Paine—organized a protest. On

December 16, 1773, a group of colonists disguised as Mohawk Indians climbed aboard tea ships in Boston Harbor and dumped 342 chests of tea overboard.

The Boston Tea Party drew a swift and tough response from Parliament and George III. In a series of laws that the colonists called the Intolerable Acts, the British closed the port of Boston. The acts no longer allowed towns to hold meetings to settle local matters. They declared that colonial officials accused of crimes had to be tried in England. They also gave British troops the right to live free of charge in the homes of colonists.

The Intolerable Acts did more to unite the colonies than any other action of the British government. In September 1774, 12 of the 13 colonies—only Georgia abstained— sent delegates to the First Continental Congress in Philadelphia to deter- mine how the colonists should respond to British policies. Among the delegates were men, including Samuel Adams, his younger cousin John

John Adams was a well- respected lawyer in Boston.

In December 1773, the Boston Tea Party set the colonies on a swifter path to the Revolution.

Adams, and Thomas Jefferson of Virginia, who wanted to break completely away from England. Others, such as Franklin, hoped to reach a compromise that would allow the colonies some form of self-government while they still maintained ties to England.

In the end, the Congress agreed to a colony-wide boycott of British goods. Committees were established to make sure all colonies followed the boycott. The delegates also issued a Declaration of Rights and Grievances. This document claimed that the colonies had the right to pass their own tax laws and denied the right of the British Parliament to govern them.

As the year 1775 began, many colonists were hopeful that an understanding could be reached with the British over the governance of the colonies. Many others, however, were determined to break free of British rule. No colony had been controlled more forcefully by the British than Massachusetts. Many of the colonists there believed that war with England was only a matter of time, and they began to prepare for battle.

Paine quickly sized up the situation in America. The whole conflict had its roots in disagreement over constitutional rights. Americans felt that England had enacted oppressive laws without colonial consent because there were no colonial representatives in Parliament. The Crown, on the other hand, maintained that the House of Commons branch of Parliament represented all subjects, anywhere in the kingdom, from England to the colonies. This "invisible" representation gave the English government the right to enact laws and levy taxes on anyone under its dominion.

Editor for Justice and Liberty

In this highly charged atmosphere, Paine's freethinking spirit found a niche. Like other craftsmen who hoped to improve their intellects, he frequented Philadelphia's many bookshops. Eventually, he struck up a friendship with the owner of one shop, Robert Aitken.

Aitken was about to start a publication with John Witherspoon, the president of the College of New Jersey, which later became Princeton University. When Aitken read Paine's writing, he asked the newcomer to become a contributing author. Soon, Aitken offered Paine the position of editor of the new *Pennsylvania Magazine*. Paine could hardly believe how events had turned in his favor. After just a few months in America, he had the most respectable job he had ever held.

In the first few issues of the magazine, published early in 1775, Paine wrote under pseudonyms such as Vox Populi, a common phrase of the time, which meant the "voice of the people." Optimistic for one of the first times in his life, he expressed hope for the future and even called for America and England to reconcile their differences. Some of Paine's pieces were informative, others lighthearted. As he had as a member of the Headstrong Club, Paine wrote essays, parables, poems, and songs.

Paine was moved by the promise of America, but he also recognized injustices, such as slavery and the oppression of women. His home was across the street from a slave auction house. When he witnessed how Africans were treated as property, he wrote essays that called the practice "monstrous" and "disgusting." In a piece titled "African Slavery in America," written in 1775, he called for abolition and said that Americans "complain so loudly of attempts to enslave them, while they hold so many hundred thousands in slavery." He signed the piece with the pen name "Justice and Humanity."

As time went on, Paine's writing grew more critical of England. One piece accused the Crown and General Thomas Gage in Boston of corruption. In another, he recounted the British mistreatment of people in India. In that nation, the British East India Company had forced Indian rulers to permit their agents to collect taxes from the people. The agents,

Thomas Gage was a target of Paine's criticism in 1775.

aided by the British army, had brought poverty and famine to millions of Indians. Paine's tone in his writing was often impudent and sarcastic. He called the king an "Honorable plunderer."

In April 1775, less than 6 months after Paine's arrival, the first shots of the American Revolution were fired on Lexington Green, between Boston and Concord, Massachusetts. Early on the morning of April 19, British troops had left Boston to destroy the colonists' military supplies and to capture Samuel Adams and John Hancock, who were staying in the area. The well-known battles of Lexington and Concord were the result of this action, and news of the events spread rapidly through the colonies.

When word of the battles reached Philadelphia, Paine's writing suddenly took a more radical turn. In "Thoughts on Defensive War," he said that liberty itself was now at stake. He suggested that further violence might be required, even though it went against his pacifist Quaker upbringing.

Paine wrote a song called "The Liberty Tree," which quickly became popular. In the North, where Bostonians rallied under the branches of a giant elm, Paine's verses were regarded as a call to arms:

> From the East to the West blow the trumpet
>   to arms,
> Thro' the land let the sound of it flee:
> Let the far and near all unite with a cheer,
> In defense of our Liberty Tree.

Thomas Paine

The first shots of the American Revolution were fired on Lexington Green early on April 19, 1775.

Not everyone appreciated Paine's ability to stir passions. His conservative publisher, Aitken, worried that the writer's politics would alienate the wealthy Loyalists who supported the Crown—and the magazine. He could not deny, however, that circulation had nearly tripled since Paine had become editor. *Pennsylvania Magazine* was now the best-selling magazine in America.

The two finally parted company in August 1775, when Paine asked for a contract that guaranteed his position, and Aitken refused. Paine was not upset to leave the job. He had plans for a much more important project.

Common Sense

By the time he left his position as editor, Paine had begun to write the pamphlet that eventually made him one of the most famous voices of the American Revolution. Since the first battle of the war, he had grown convinced that the time to claim independence was at hand. His pamphlet called for the American colonies to sever ties with England completely. It was a bold action, and his friends told him to be careful with his words, because they could be considered treasonous. The majority of people in America were not ready for such a revolutionary step. Delegates in Congress discussed the pros and cons of such action, but most still hoped to find a way to make amends with England.

For Paine, compromise was out of the question.

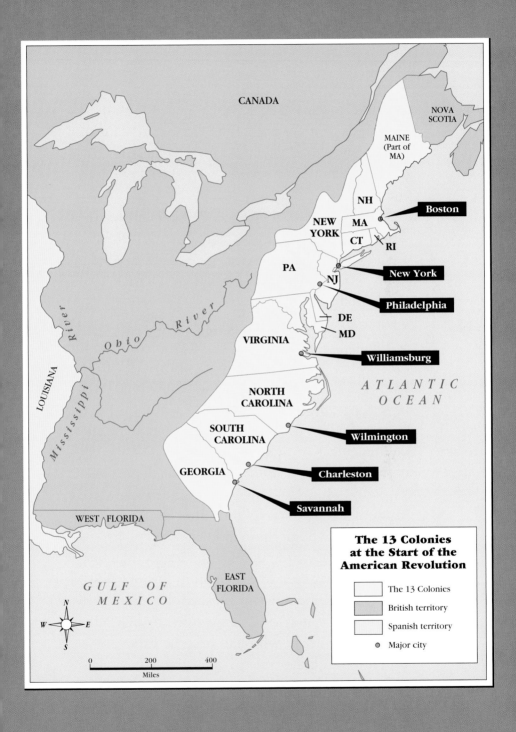

CANADA

NOVA
SCOTIA

MAINE
(Part of
MA)

NH

NEW
YORK

MA

CT

RI

Boston

PA

NJ

New York

Philadelphia

DE

MD

VIRGINIA

Williamsburg

*ATLANTIC
OCEAN*

NORTH
CAROLINA

SOUTH
CAROLINA

Wilmington

GEORGIA

Charleston

Savannah

Ohio River

River

LOUISIANA

Mississippi

WEST FLORIDA

EAST
FLORIDA

*GULF OF
MEXICO*

N
W E
S

0   200   400
Miles

The 13 Colonies
at the Start of the
American Revolution

The 13 Colonies

British territory

Spanish territory

● Major city

When he considered the colonies' problems with the Crown, he thought it made no sense to back down: How could a gigantic, prosperous, and energetic continent be ruled by a small island thousands of miles away?, he wondered. The king of that island had also used force against his own subjects. That alone seemed to make a complete break necessary.

As he wrote his new piece, Paine intended to show people what he saw as the plain truth: There was no reason for America's obedience to England. Paine planned to ask Americans to use their "Common Sense."

Paine wrote throughout the fall of 1775. It seemed to him as if everything in his life had led up to this one piece of writing—his father's distrust of authority, his own alliance with freethinking religious sects, his discussions at the Headstrong Club, his poverty and hard labor, his concern for the common man, and his ability to preach and persuade. Paine drew on his reading and studies of politics, his experience of corruption in England, and his keen knowledge of the Bible as he wrote draft after draft.

As he brought all those influences and experiences together, Paine wrote in his usual logical manner. The words, sparked by rebellion in Boston, flowed out. By December, he was finished. He showed his manuscript, a small book he wanted to call *Plain Truth*, to Franklin, who had become firmly committed to independence after the battles of Lexington and Concord. Paine also asked Samuel

COMMON SENSE;

ADDRESSED TO THE

INHABITANTS

OF

AMERICA,

ON THE FOLLOWING INTERESTING

SUBJECTS:

I. Of the Origin and Design of Government in general, with concise Remarks on the English Constitution.

II. Of Monarchy and Hereditary Succession.

III. Thoughts on the present State of American Affairs.

IV. Of the present ability of America, with some miscellaneous Reflections.

A NEW EDITION, with several Additions in the Body of the Work. To which is added an APPENDIX; together with an Address to the People called QUAKERS.

By THOMAS PAINE,

SECRETARY FOR FOREIGN AFFAIRS TO CONGRESS IN THE AMERICAN WAR, AND AUTHOR OF THE RIGHTS OF MAN, &c. &c.

Man knows no Master save creating HEAVEN,
Or those whom choice and common Good ordain.

THOMSON.

PHILADELPHIA:

PRINTED AND SOLD BY W. AND T. BRADFORD.

M, DCC, XCI.

Common Sense was a plea by Paine for the colonies to reject British control.

Adams and another member of Congress, Benjamin Rush, to review the work. They made only minor changes. Rush convinced Paine to change the title of the piece to *Common Sense*. Printer Robert Bell agreed to publish it. On January, 10, 1776, the 48-page booklet *Common Sense* went on sale for two shillings, about 10 cents in today's money.

The pamphlet found an immediate audience. Its first printing sold out in two weeks. In a few months, more than 150,000 copies had been sold. Farmers, tradesmen, housewives, soldiers, and politicians read it. The many colonists who could not read had others read it aloud to them. All of them grasped its meaning.

Bold Statements

Paine did not mince words in *Common Sense*. He knew that he was speaking boldly in his work, but the cause that he supported was one that extended beyond the colonies. "The cause of America is in a great measure the cause of all mankind," he wrote in the introduction.

Paine began *Common Sense* with the subject of government, which he called "a necessary evil." The best government, he said, is that which has "the least expense and greatest benefit." He described his ideal government as one that arose from the people.

Paine then contrasted his ideal government with monarchy, a form of government that he called "exceedingly ridiculous." A king is a contradiction, said Paine, because the "state of a king shuts him from the world, yet the business of a king requires him to know it thoroughly." Paine said kings are "absurd and useless." What made monarchy worse, according to Paine, was the practice of succession—rulers who passed their reign on to their children. Because monarchy only protected the rights of the few, he reasoned, it ruined the whole country. "Monarchy and succession have laid . . . the world in blood and ashes," he wrote.

Paine then addressed the main point of his pamphlet, his reason why the colonies should separate from England. Though many colonists regarded England as a mother country, he said, a true parent country would protect its subjects. Instead, England had persecuted them "with the cruelty of a monster." He wrote, "Shame upon her conduct. Even brutes do not devour their young; nor savages make war upon their families." After Lexington and Concord, to reconcile with such a monster "was a dream that has passed away," he wrote.

★

In February 1776, John Paul Jones was in Philadelphia where he trained the crew of the American warship *Alfred*.

★

Paine next described his own personal turning point that occurred when he heard news of battles. "The moment the event of that day was made known, I rejected the hardened, sullen tempered Pharaoh of England for ever; and disdain the wretch, that with the pretended title of FATHER OF HIS PEOPLE can unfeelingly hear of their slaughter, and composedly sleep with their blood

47

With the publication of *Common Sense*, Paine became an instant celebrity in the colonies.

upon his soul."

Paine went on to address those readers who were reluctant to break away. "If there is any true cause of fear respecting independence it is because no plan is yet laid down. Men do not see their way out. Wherefore, as an opening into that business I offer the following hint." He then outlined in great detail a system of government created by a document he called a "continental charter," in which colonies were divided into districts, and representatives were elected from each district.

The representatives would meet yearly to enact laws. A president would be elected each year to preside over the legislature.

Paine next emphasized how important it was to create a navy for the new country. He wrote a lengthy description of the many natural resources that the colonies possessed that would enable them to defend themselves. "No country on the globe is so happily situated, so internally capable of raising a fleet as America. Tar, timber, iron, and cordage are her natural produce. We need go abroad for nothing." He wanted to reassure doubtful colonists that the colonies could actually win a war against the most powerful military empire in the world.

Paine knew that the establishment of independence would require war. Yet he stressed that the war would not be one of conquest, but one to defend America. He tried to reassure readers who feared the power of Britain that a revolution was winnable. "Our present numbers are sufficient to repel the force of all the world," he wrote. America was not in debt. It had plenty of able-bodied fighters as well as resources. "Resolution is our inherent character, and courage hath never yet forsaken us. Wherefore, what is it that we want?"

To win the war would take more than resources, though, and more than courage. Paine stated that the colonies would need to pull together to make independence real. "It is not in numbers but in unity, that our great strength lies," Paine wrote.

In the final portion of *Common Sense*, Paine returned to his core belief that the time was right for revolution. "The sun never shined on a cause of greater worth.... Now is the seedtime of continental union, faith, and honor," he wrote.

Chapter 3

"TIMES THAT TRY MEN'S SOULS"

*C*ommon *Sense* did more for America than Paine ever imagined. Though others had expressed similar ideas, Paine's book addressed a wider audience because it was written in language that common people could understand. Paine called for a new order, a popular democracy, that included the working class—tradesmen, farmers, and laborers, not just intellectuals and property owners.

OPPOSITE: As the main meeting place of the Continental Congress, Philadelphia was the center of the American Revolution.

Common Sense was read from Maine to the Carolinas. It encouraged Americans to think of themselves not as inhabitants of 13 separate colonies, but as a united whole. Paine gave the people hope that they could do something that had never been done before—form their own government.

Many people considered Paine the true voice of the Revolution. The bold language and colorful imagery in his writing changed the minds of many people who were undecided about the right course for America. People began to understand that they could only progress economically through independence, which would allow the tax money they spent to be used to their overall benefit. The time to separate was now, Paine insisted. If they waited, England's tyranny would expand and they would be powerless subjects forever. Moreover, American taxes would go to pay for tyranny rather than public good. Paine's sense of urgency inflamed the hearts of the Patriots.

Soldiers who fought in the North passed around copies of *Common Sense*, while General George Washington struggled to shape a new Continental army from a jumble of local militias. Many soldiers still were not fully sure why they should agree to fight. As they read Paine's pamphlet aloud around their campfires, it began "working a wonderful change in the minds of many men," said Washington.

Delegates to the Second Continental Congress, which met through late 1775 and into 1776, disagreed about the ideas in *Common Sense* at first. On Paine's side were influential men such as the Adamses, Rush, and Franklin. On the other side, those who sided with the Crown, the Tories, were outraged. A Tory who used the pen name "Cato" published attacks against *Common Sense* in the *Pennsylvania Gazette* and other newspapers.

In letters signed "The Forester," Paine wrote rebuttals through the winter and early spring of 1776. By that time, more colonial assemblies began to write resolutions that echoed Paine's call in *Common Sense*. They advised their delegates in Philadelphia to break with England. In June 1776, the Congress formed a committee to draft a document to declare the nation's independence. Jefferson was selected to write it, with assistance from a committee that included Franklin and John Adams. The Declaration of Independence was approved by delegates on July 2. Within a month, it had been printed and distributed widely.

In the Service of America

By the summer of 1776, Paine had revised *Common Sense* a number of times. Demand for the pamphlet grew faster than copies could be printed. Printers all over the colonies printed their own editions, because there were no copyright laws that protected a writer's work until 1790. Paine did not object to others making money from his work. He wanted the piece to be distributed as widely as possible. It is believed that 1 in 5 colonists read *Common Sense*.

53

As popular as *Common Sense* was, Paine never kept any money from its sale. Any profits he made went to the purchase of supplies for the Continental army. Although he had become well known throughout the colonies as a leader of the independence movement, he did not have a way to make a living. At the height of his popularity, the money he had saved from when he worked on the *Pennsylvania Magazine* was almost gone.

Shortly after the Declaration of Independence was read to the public, Paine followed his deep commitment to the American cause and enlisted in the Pennsylvania militia. He accepted a position as secretary to General Daniel Roberdeau. The group was a "flying camp." Soldiers signed on for short periods and were trained to rush quickly to where they were needed at front lines, then disbanded after the battle was over.

Soon after Paine joined the militia in July 1776, they marched to Perth Amboy, New Jersey, across the mouth of the Hudson River from New York City. Their mission was to thwart a British takeover of Manhattan Island. They were to assist Washington, who had most of his army stationed across New York Harbor on Manhattan. As Roberdeau's men watched from the west, hundreds of ships made their way up the harbor. More than 30,000 British troops disembarked at Staten Island, south of Washington's encampment. The sight of the huge number of British soldiers overwhelmed the militia who had not anticipated that they

Benjamin Franklin, John Adams, Thomas Jefferson, and two other delegates formed the committee that drafted the Declaration of Independence.

would face the full might of the British army. Many militiamen deserted the ranks.

In camp, Paine distributed and read *Common Sense* in an attempt to rally his companions' spirits. By September, the men had not seen action, and many had completed their enlistment period. During that time, the British forces under General William Howe had left Staten Island and soundly defeated American troops on Long Island. Washington had removed his forces from Long Island and moved his entire army to the northern end of Manhattan Island, which gave control of lower Manhattan and the entire New York Harbor to the British. The volunteers had remained out of the bloody month of fighting, unable to secure transport across the harbor now guarded by British warships. Most militiamen gladly returned home rather then face the British army.

Paine left his unit and moved north to join the Continental army, which was encamped on both sides of the Hudson River. At Fort Lee on the Palisades, the west banks of the Hudson, he served as an aide to General Nathanael Greene. While there, Paine gathered intelligence for Greene and wrote reports for newspapers back in Philadelphia.

While Paine remained at Fort Lee, the situation across the river grew rapidly worse for the Continental army. On October 12, British ships sailed up the East River into Long Island Sound. During the night, a large force of redcoats landed in the Bronx. Howe planned to trap Washington

In August 1776, more than 30,000 British troops landed on Long Island in New York.

and his patriot troops at Harlem Heights, on the northern end of Manhattan Island.

To avoid the trap, Washington left several thousand men at Fort Washington on the island's northern end and retreated across to the mainland, moving northwest away from the British. Howe followed Washington and caught up with him at White Plains on October 28, 1776.

At White Plains, Washington placed his main army on high ground to the north and east with about 1,600 troops to the west on Chatterton's Hill. Howe attacked the troops on Chatterton's

57

Hill. The charge was disastrous for the British—about 230 British soldiers lost their lives compared to about 100 Americans. The British loss, however, was only a temporary setback.

While the British regrouped, Washington withdrew his army to a position north of White Plains. When Howe learned of that move, he made plans to draw Washington into an attack, and sent his troops down the east bank of the Hudson River to Dobbs Ferry. From there, he could attack Fort Washington or cross over to New Jersey and destroy Fort Lee before he headed to Philadelphia. Any path Howe chose would require a response from the Patriots.

Washington decided to divide his army. He left General Charles Lee with a large force of men north of Howe. He then posted some soldiers farther north to guard the city of Peekskill, a gateway to the upper Hudson River. Finally, with about 2,000 soldiers, Washington crossed the lower Hudson into New Jersey and placed his men in position to stop a British advance toward Philadelphia.

General Charles Lee commanded Fort Washington in New York City.

By mid-November, after the battles around New York City,

Thomas Paine

Paine knew that the prospects for the Continental army looked bleak. Yet to rouse people's hopes in Philadelphia, his reports made it sound as though the American retreat was only part of a grand strategy for victory.

Paine's reports were far from the truth. On November 16, British soldiers, commanded by General Charles Cornwallis, surrounded Fort Washington and captured about 3,000 men, as well as cannons and gunpowder. From his viewpoint high atop the Palisades, Paine watched as Fort Washington fell.

The British at once began to gather for an attack on Fort Lee. On the night of November 18, Greene saw that he could not defend the fort against the British forces. American reinforcements had not reached Fort Lee as requested. As enemy forces pressed in, Greene's men left hot cooking pots on the fire and fled through the rain and muck to join Washington's fleeing force. The Patriots retreated so quickly that they left behind a supply of ammunition and weapons.

A Time of Crisis

Paine marched south through New Jersey with the retreating American troops. By that point, Paine and many others who had seen the British in battle realized that Washington's inexperienced troops had little chance against the well-trained enemy. The Patriots' muskets sometimes failed to fire. Their uniforms and shoes were in tatters. The

59

Hessian soldiers were feared by the untrained American troops.

British were not only better trained, but they had more troops, including thousands of Hessians—hired professional soldiers from Germany.

When the American soldiers reached Trenton, Paine received permission from his officers to return to Philadelphia. As he put it, he knew that "the country was in a state of despair." For weeks, without paper, he had written on the dried leather of split drumskins discarded by the army's drummers. Paine was consumed with new ideas for a paper that he wanted to publish. He felt the army and the people desperately needed to have their spirits restored.

Paine walked 35 miles back to Philadelphia alone. When he arrived in early December 1776, he found the city nearly deserted. Congress had moved to Baltimore, Maryland, in the belief that the British might soon overtake Philadelphia. Tories waited eagerly to welcome the redcoats.

In little more than a week, Paine composed

Colonial Philadelphia

Race Street

Betsy Ross House

Arch Street

Free Quaker Meeting House

Christ Church Burial Ground

Christ Church

Church Street

Market Street

Benjamin Franklin House

Graff House

7th Street

6th Street

5th Street

4th Street

3rd Street

2nd Street

Chestnut Street

City Hall

Pennsylvania State House (Indepndence Hall)

Carpenters' Hall

Sansom Street

City Tavern

Walnut Street

St. Joseph's Church

Chancellor Street

N
W E
S

Willings Alley

0   250   500
Feet

Locust Street

Much of the activity of the Contiental Congress took place in an area of Phiadelphia known as "Center City" (shown).

another of his most famous works, which he wrote in a "passion of patriotism," he said. A week before Christmas, his paper, called *The American Crisis*, appeared in the *Pennsylvania Journal*. Four days later, it was published as a pamphlet that aimed to renew the inspiration of Americans for the struggle ahead. *The American Crisis* would be followed by more than a dozen such papers over the course of the war, but none had such a memorable opening as the lines that became some of the most famous of the American Revolution:

> *These are the times that try men's souls. The summer soldier and the sunshine patriot will, in this crisis, shrink from the service of their country; but he that stands it now, deserves the love and thanks of man and woman. Tyranny, like hell, is not easily conquered; yet we have this consolation with us, that the harder the conflict, the more glorious the triumph.*

Paine reminded readers that God was on the side of the Americans, who had "sought to avoid the calamities of war." A king who enslaved people, Paine said, could never expect heaven to help him.

Paine beseeched people not to panic or abandon the cause. In relating his firsthand experience of the army's retreat in New Jersey, he sought to quell fears as he explained that the British commander, Howe, had not conquered anything. In fact, Howe "committed a great error in generalship," Paine said. He pointed out that a competent general would have sent his forces against the lightly defended area at Perth Amboy, where Paine's militia unit had been stationed. From there, Paine explained, Howe could have captured the large store of Patriot weapons in New Brunswick, New Jersey, and cut off the Continental army on its march across New Jersey, rather than chasing it. Paine said that he could only imagine one reason why those events did not come to pass: "If we believe the power of hell to be limited, we must likewise believe that the[y] . . . are under some providential control."

Paine next had scathing words for those who supported the Crown. The middle colonies of New York, New Jersey, Pennsylvania, Maryland, and Delaware, he said, were "infested with Tories."
He asked, "And what is a Tory? Good GOD! what is he? . . . Every Tory is a coward." Howe was mistaken if he thought the Tories would help him, he said. They might take up useless opinions, but they did not have the courage to take up arms. "Self-interested fear is the foundation of Toryism," Paine wrote. Though a Tory "may be cruel, [he] never can be brave." If the Tories were to aid Howe in any way, Paine said, he wished that the Americans would "expel them from the continent."

Paine then repeated that independence from the British was the only choice. He claimed that his

★

By December 1776, the American ship *Alfred*, under Captain John Paul Jones, had captured 8 British merchant ships.

★

63

view was popular and widespread: "Not a man lives on the continent but fully believes that a separation must some time or other finally take place. I am as confident, as I am that God governs the world, that America will never be happy till she gets clear of foreign dominion ... for, though the flame of liberty may sometimes cease to shine, the coal never can expire."

Through *The American Crisis*, Paine aimed to gather support for the Continental army, not just in principle, but in recruits. Real bravery was on the side of the Patriots, Paine asserted. In his conclusion, he said that soldiers were heroes, and those who had retreated had done so "with a manly and martial spirit" and now needed reinforcement. The men of the army wished only "that the country would turn out and help them to drive the enemy back." Paine used all his powers of persuasion to encourage enlistment:

"I call ... on every state; up and help us, lay your shoulders to the wheel.... Let it be told to the future world that in the depth of winter, when nothing but hope and virtue could survive, that the city and the country, alarmed at one common danger, came forth to meet and to repulse it. Say not that thousands are gone, turn out your tens of thousands .... 'Tis the business of little minds to shrink, but he whose heart is firm and whose conscience approves his conduct will pursue his principles unto death."

New Crises and an Appointment

Paine's words were designed not only to encourage enlistment but also to rekindle the courage of men who were already in the army. Two days after the pamphlet's publication, Washington led his troops across the Delaware River. The men were hungry, cold, barely clothed, and sick. Somehow, the general needed to convince them that they could recross the river and defeat the Hessians at Trenton in a surprise attack.

After he read Paine's piece, Washington called his men together and read aloud parts of *The American Crisis*. Paine's words reassured the soldiers that they were not forgotten, that their hardship was not in vain.

Paine's stirring words helped carry the day. On December 26, Washington's troops surprised the

Washington took a great risk by leading his troops across the icy Delaware River in the early morning hours of December 26, 1776.

groggy Hessians at Trenton, where they had spent all of Christmas day eating and drinking. On January 3, 1777, the Americans won another victory over Cornwallis at Princeton. These long-awaited triumphs instilled hope and confidence in the army.

On January 13, Paine wrote a second *American Crisis* pamphlet. This one was a response to a call Howe had made for the Americans to surrender. Howe offered to pardon any American who laid down his arms. Paine scoffed at Howe and the British king, whom he called a "monster." He wrote that the Patriots would never reconcile with Britain. Paine also became the first person to used the term "United States of America" to describe the former colonies.

Paine paid to print this paper and again refused all profits from its sale. He called on friends he had met through Franklin to help him secure a salaried position. In response, they had Paine appointed secretary to a commission to meet with Iroquois tribes, who had taken the side of the British and were attacking colonists in the northern areas of Pennsylvania. In early 1777, he went to the town of Easton to work out a treaty. The treaty was signed by only 3 of the 6 groups of Iroquois, but Paine earned enough money in his role to pay his debts.

In March, Congress returned from Baltimore and began to look for ways to secure money from powers overseas to finance the war. On April 17,

John Adams surprised Paine when he nominated him to serve as the paid secretary to a newly created foreign affairs committee. Paine was confirmed, and since he had not profited from his written work, he felt that the position was an honor that was due him for his efforts to sustain the spirit of independence.

Just two days after his appointment, Paine, 40, wrote a third *American Crisis* paper. In it, he urged the Pennsylvania assembly to require Americans to take an oath of loyalty to "independence." He suggested that those who would not take the oath be subjected to a high property tax. He attacked Tories, who were interested only in "avarice, villainy, and personal power."

Late in the summer of 1777, British generals Henry Clinton and Cornwallis had landed troops at Delaware Bay. The huge British force began to march toward Philadelphia. Paine wrote dispatches to Franklin, who was in Paris, and informed him that the British had landed south of the city. They planned to capture Philadelphia, which had resumed its normal bustling pace once the Continental Congress had returned from Baltimore earlier in the year.

Henry Clinton was one of the most unpopular commanders among British troops.

Meanwhile, Washington prepared to stop the British advance. On September 11, the Americans marched about 25 miles southwest of Philadelphia to confront Howe at Brandywine Creek in southeastern Pennsylvania. There, the British general outflanked Washington and forced him to retreat. The Americans suffered about 1,200 casualties. About 600 British troops were killed or wounded.

The road to Philadelphia was suddenly wide open for the British, and residents began to flee. In a single day, Paine quickly wrote a fourth *American Crisis* paper. In it, he tried to bolster morale and urged people to defend Philadelphia. "Men who are sincere in defending their freedom," he wrote, would be concerned and rise "with additional vigor; the glow of hope, courage, and fortitude will, in a little time, supply the place of every inferior passion, and kindle the whole heart into heroism." Congress stood its ground for a week, but then fled on September 18 to York, Pennsylvania. By then, one-third of the population of Philadelphia had also fled.

For the next two weeks, Howe tried to corner Washington's troops around Philadelphia. Washington avoided a direct battle; instead, he sent small units to strike at the British in isolated camps. In early October, Washington attacked Germantown, a British camp 7 miles from Philadelphia. The element of surprise almost led to an American victory, but American soldiers became confused in a thick fog and began to fire on one another. Finally, on October 19, Howe and the British forces entered Philadelphia.

Paine stayed until the last minute. Alarms sounded on the morning of October 19, to alert residents that the British had entered the city. Paine's position as a foreign affairs secretary obliged him to safeguard official committee documents, pertaining to relations with France, that were in his care. He packed them in a trunk and sent them north to Trenton on an army supply wagon.

Paine then proceeded to the home of a friend across the Delaware River near Bordentown, New Jersey. A few days later, he went in search of Washington. On the way to the general's temporary head-quarters outside of Philadelphia, he saw many wounded soldiers along the roads, slowly making their way from the defeat at Germantown. In camp, Paine met with Greene and Washington and explained that before he left Philadelphia, he had been requested by the Pennsylvania Executive Council to act as an official observer of Washington's army and to compose reports of the actions the army took in the colony.

By October, the army was bogged down in torrential rains, and there was little to report. The only good news during that time came from New York, where Patriots under General Henry Gates and General Benedict Arnold had defeated British General John Burgoyne at Saratoga. This victory

★

In late September 1777, British infantry attacked sleeping American soldiers with bayonets in the village of Paoli, Pennsylvania, killing 50 men and wounding hundreds.

★

Thousands of Patriots died from cold and disease during the winter at Valley Forge.

gave Americans control of the Hudson River and New England. Saratoga became more than a military triumph in the course of the war. It was the key battle that convinced France to enter the war on the side of the Americans.

By late fall, the weather around Philadelphia had turned bitter cold. Washington's men prepared to make camp for the winter at Valley Forge, about 20 miles outside of Philadelphia. Paine made notes for a report to the executive council as the troops built primitive huts for shelter. Once the army was in camp, Paine saw that his task for the council was through for the winter. He eventually made his way to York, where Congress held its meetings.

During the winter, Paine lived with a friend in nearby Lancaster, Pennsylvania. Some historians have criticized him for staying close to a warm fire while Washington's men froze and starved at Valley Forge, but he had to be close to Congress to carry out his post as secretary in foreign affairs. He hoped the job would one day develop into a more responsible, higher-paid position.

Chapter 4

FROM RUIN
TO REPAIR

Paine could be a clearheaded, inspired writer who rallied a nation. Yet he could also be overly aggressive in his beliefs and say more than was wise. These contrasts in his personality led him to commit a terrible mistake.

Paine often held an overly important view of his own job as the secretary for the committee of foreign affairs. He sometimes referred to himself as the "Secretary of Foreign Affairs." In fact, he was a recording secretary and clerk. Paine's duties were to take notes at committee meetings, file papers, and draft outgoing dispatches. One of the most important requirements of his job was that he maintain a strict code of silence about all information that he heard, read, or communicated in his work. Failure to do so could cost him his job.

OPPOSITE: French troops landed in Rhode Island in 1780 to aid the Continental army.

In his work, Paine had access to many secret government files and letters, most of which involved sensitive foreign issues, particularly the ways in which the Americans obtained financial support from other countries for the war. When Paine took the position, he swore an oath not to disclose confidential matters of state. He broke this oath, however, and the mistake caused a scandal for Congress and its foreign ally, France.

Profiteers and Patriots

The scandal involved the French government and an American delegate from Connecticut named Silas Deane. In 1776, Congress had appointed Deane, a wealthy merchant, to go to France to secure war materials for the American army. Because America had few funds to pay for the supplies, Deane was to offer American raw materials and tobacco in trade after the war, rather than cash. In return for undertaking the mission, Congress agreed to let Deane profit from any future trade arrangements that were made between the two countries. This arrangement appealed to Deane, who lived in an area of Connecticut that was well known for its tobacco.

Because France did not want its support of America made public at that time, Deane was required to pose as a private merchant and deal with the French in secret. France feared that England might declare war if it suspected that France supported America with arms or funds.

Silas Deane (center) was a wealthy New England merchant who dealt secretly with the French.

Despite this risk, France was happy to help America against the British. The French had lost much territory in North America to England in the French and Indian War, and King Louis XVI wanted England to lose the new war with America. To assist the American cause, the French king made a secret gift of a half a million livres, a large amount of money, to America.

Because France and England were not at war, the money could not be sent overseas openly. It had to be used to buy supplies, which could then be shipped to America. To take care of the purchase and transport of supplies, Louis XVI hired an agent to set up a false private company, funded by the king's gift. That agent, Pierre-Augustin Caron de Beaumarchais, had an eye for personal gain. He used part of the king's gift to buy cheap gunpowder, then charged 5 times its cost against the king's money and pocketed the difference. He also gathered free cast-off muskets from the French arsenal and listed a high price on them, again to pocket money.

Meanwhile, in early 1777, Deane had made a separate arrangement with the French— Beaumarchais included—to provide American soldiers with shoes, socks, blankets, shovels, axes, tents, weapons, and ammunition. Those supplies were shipped to America on ships hired by Beaumarchais. The supplies were used by Patriots in their victory at Saratoga in October 1777.

As time went on, questions were raised about whether Deane and Beaumarchais were profiting from the funds that had been given by Louis XVI. Arthur Lee, an American minister stationed in France, suspected underhanded deals.

In late 1777, Congress received a bill from Beaumarchais's business for a shocking 4.5 million livres. Beaumarchais had not only pocketed the king's money, he had submitted the overcharges to Congress after he had used up the gift. Delegates immediately suspected Beaumarchais, and that suspicion spread to Deane, since he was also involved in securing supplies. Deane was recalled to Philadelphia immediately.

Deane was slow to return, and when he did, he brought no paperwork with him. He arrived in the summer of 1778. By that time, France had signed a formal alliance with America, and Deane was on the same ship as the first French ambassador to the United States, Conrad Gérard.

Deane, who had not been paid for his services, now faced accusations of profiteering and corruption. He claimed he had no knowledge of how Beaumarchais had arrived at the huge bill, and repeatedly pleaded for a chance to clear his name. When he was not allowed to argue his innocence before Congress, he wrote a letter to the newspapers to defend himself, and blasted Congress in the process.

Paine became involved in the affair because his job enabled him to read secret papers about Deane's case. He was therefore well acquainted with the issues involved, and they infuriated him. Like many people, Paine—who made no profit from his writing—resented the lavish lifestyles led by merchants while soldiers went barefoot and wore rags. Even farmers in the colonies had

★

In late June 1778, British and American forces fought the last battle of the Revolution in the North, at Monmouth, New Jersey.

★

While troops suffered with little food at Valley Forge, some farmers sold their food to the British in Philadelphia.

engaged in the practice of profiteering when they sold their food to the British for high prices during the winter of 1777, while Patriots starved in Valley Forge. Americans had been asked to sacrifice for the war effort, yet some people seemed to be far better off than ever, Paine concluded.

The Silas Deane Affair, as it came to be known, drove a wedge between members of Congress. Some delegates were outraged at Deane's suspected activity as a profiteer. Other delegates were themselves wealthy merchants who stood to benefit from trade with France. Deane's powerful friends in Congress spoke out in support of him. Arguments flared over private business versus government business.

Thomas Paine

This division came at a time when the war was far from over. If the Revolution was to be won, Congress needed to be united, not divided, Paine thought. Its members did not need to be discredited or disrespected by Deane.

When Deane publicly criticized Congress, Paine could not keep silent. As a pamphleteer, he knew how to air his patriotic thoughts in the newspapers. Paine responded to Deane's letter with a series of letters in December 1778, which he signed "*Common Sense*." This time, Paine wrote carelessly. In one letter, he mentioned that the money the French king had put in Beaumarchais's trust had been a gift to America. Paine could only have gained that information from classified official papers. To write about it in the press violated his oath of secrecy.

The new French ambassador was shocked and embarrassed. Paine's letters alerted England to the fact that France had helped America's war effort before a treaty of alliance was signed in 1778. The ambassador demanded that Congress take action against Paine. America desperately needed France's help in the war, and did not want to offend the French.

Paine was ordered to appear before a session of Congress to be questioned. Paine told Congress that his intentions had been honorable. He had only wanted "to preserve the public from error," and "to support . . . the just authority of the representatives of the people, and to . . . cement the union . . . between this country and France." In his

Pierre-Augustin Caron de Beaumarchais

Although he played a minor role in the American Revolution, Pierre-Augustin Caron de Beaumarchais was one of the most accomplished men of his time. He was born in 1732, the same year as George Washington, and was trained by his father to be a watchmaker. At age 19, he invented a clock mechanism that brought him a great deal of money.

Beaumarchais was also a talented musician who played several instruments. At 27, he became the harp teacher to the daughters of King Louis XV. His inside view of the lives of French royalty and nobility made him decide to write comic plays that ridiculed the pretenses of the upper class. His two best-known works were the *The Barber of Seville* and *The Marriage of Figaro*. The famous composers Rossini and Mozart composed operas based on the plays.

Beaumarchais was an early supporter of the cause of American independence and was eager to aid in the secret plan to secure supplies for the Patriots. He also saw an opportunity to make money, which was important since he had made and spent an enormous amount of money by the time he reached middle age.

Throughout the American Revolution, Beaumarchais denied that he was a profiteer. When the French Revolution began in the 1780s, Beaumarchais was banished from the country because of his connection to the royal family. He eventually returned to Paris, where he died in 1799—the same year as George Washington. Beaumarchais's descendants continued to insist on payment of the bill that Beaumarchais had presented to the Congress. In 1832, Congress voted to give the family a grant of land in Louisiana.

A fanciful drawing of Beaumarchais shows him in the costume of a character in his play, *The Marriage of Figaro*.

passion, however, Paine had revealed exactly what France and America had both wanted to keep quiet.

In January 1779, Deane's supporters called for Paine to be fired. Humiliated that he might become the first person ever discharged by the government, Paine quickly resigned. Congress officially denied that the king of France had sent any military supplies to America before the 1778 alliance. It refused to pay Beaumarchais's bill.

After Paine resigned, he shut himself away in his lodgings in Philadelphia and began to drink heavily. He fell ill for several months due to alcohol-related causes. When he regained his health, he refused to let the Deane Affair drop. No longer employed by the government, he wrote freely and published many letters and essays in the press to defend his character.

Although some colonial leaders continued to make Paine the focus of attention for his violations of his oath, his letters kept the heat on Deane and other profiteers. The negative public opinion of the many merchants, manufacturers, and farmers who made money off the war grew so intense that, in Philadelphia, militiamen seized and jailed 20 of the men who had become wealthiest from profiteering. In time, two states outlawed the use of government deals by delegates for personal profit.

Congress never acted against Deane, who moved to Europe. As more information about the extent of profiteering became public, some who had once supported Deane believed Paine had been right to rebuke him. In 1789, Silas Deane died in poverty while in Europe.

A Turnaround

In July 1779, Paine was able to secure a low-paying job with a Quaker merchant. The tide of public opinion became more favorable for him when his friends held a public rally of support outside the State House in Philadelphia. In November, they found him a clerk's position with the Pennsylvania General Assembly. In this capacity, he helped write the preamble to laws that would eventually make Pennsylvania the first state to abolish slavery in 1780.

★

In September 1779, the *Bonhomme Richard* under Captain John Paul Jones defeated the British ship *Serapis* in the largest naval battle of the Revolution.

★

Paine soon re-entered political writing with his former enthusiasm. Washington's men still needed financial support, and Paine called on wealthy merchants to donate money to an account for the army. He even pledged a good deal of his own small savings. The account grew to become the Bank of Pennsylvania, and later, the Bank of North America.

On July 4, 1780, the University of Pennsylvania recognized the service Paine had given America and awarded him an honorary Master of Arts degree. Because Paine had had no formal education past the age of 13, this tribute bolstered his spirits.

During the summer and fall, Paine wrote new *American Crisis* papers and other pamphlets. In one, titled *Public Good*, he called for a convention

83

to draft a constitution for America. It planted the seed for the Constitutional Convention that took place in Philadelphia in 1787.

In another *American Crisis* paper, Paine suggested that America seek more aid from France. Congress took his advice and chose a delegate, but to Paine's disappointment, Colonel John Laurens was selected. Paine had hoped to be named to the post, and perhaps make amends for the trouble he had caused. Laurens asked Paine to join him as his unofficial secretary—an unpaid assignment. Paine, who was eager to go abroad, agreed. In early 1781, Paine journeyed to France with Laurens. The Atlantic crossing was treacherous, but their mission was successful. Laurens and Paine returned to America with 2.5 million livres in aid and shiploads of supplies.

During the visit, Paine was treated as a hero by many of the French, and his presence on the mission was largely responsible for France's willingness to provide money and supplies. A French newspaper wrote of Paine's work that it "must in the opinion of the best judges place the author in the highest ranks of literature."

Writer for Hire

Paine had hardly a penny left to his name when he returned to Philadelphia. For the next year, he was unable to find anyone who would pay for his writing. A number of people still looked down on him because he had revealed government secrets.

His reputation suffered so greatly from his involvement in the Silas Deane Affair that when a friend nominated him for membership in the American Philosophical Society, Franklin's daughter Sarah blocked his election. "There never was a man less beloved in a place than Paine is in this," she said. "The most rational thing he could have done would have been to have died the instant he had finished his *Common Sense*, for he never again will have it in his power to leave the world with so much credit."

For the present, Paine's prospects looked bleak. He requested that Congress hire him as an army correspondent, but it did not see the need. The war was in its final phase. By October 1781, Washington had cornered Cornwallis and his troops in Virginia and forced them to surrender. The rest of the English army was confined in New York, unable to move.

Paine wrote directly to Washington. He complained that he had done a generous and honorable duty for America, yet the nation now neglected him. Washington arranged with Congress's finance manager, Robert Morris, and the head of foreign

As Congress's finance manager, Robert Morris hired Paine as a government writer.

85

affairs, Robert Livingston, to hire Paine as a government writer. He was charged with "informing the people and rousing them to action." He would be paid a yearly sum from a secret fund, backed by the wealthy Morris.

Paine went to work immediately. In *Thoughts on the Peace, and the probable Advantages thereof,* published in 1783, he reminded his readers that the American Revolution had opened "a new system of . . . civilization." He returned to an idea he had first put forth in *Common Sense,* as he explained that everything was changed by the Revolution. America's victory would set an example for the whole world, he claimed. "The true idea of a great nation," he wrote, "extends and promotes the principles of universal society."

Paine's idea of a universal society extended beyond America. He began to refer to himself as a "citizen of the world." He believed that the struggle for liberty was a global one. Franklin had once said, "Where liberty is, there is my country." Paine had replied, "Where liberty is not, there is my country."

On a number of occasions, Paine expressed an interest in going back to Europe. He was popular in France and thought he could make a better base of operations there for his political writing. The American diplomats in France, however,—Franklin and Laurens—were not eager to have him any closer. His writing was bitterly anti-British, and they were in delicate negotiations with England to end the war formally.

Thomas Paine

The Revolution Ends

In 1783, news came from Europe that England had agreed to a peace treaty. The war between England and America had finally come to an end. Thomas Paine wrote his thirteenth *American Crisis* paper. "The times that tried men's souls are now over," he wrote, "and the greatest and completest revolution the world ever knew, gloriously and happily accomplished."

Once again, he reminded his readers of the global importance of America's success. The Revolution, he wrote, "contributed more to enlighten the world, and a ... spirit of freedom and liberality among mankind than any human event ... that ever preceded it." Paine warned that the new union must now be strengthened. As usual, his writing was filled with patriotic enthusiasm: "Our union well and wisely regulated and cemented, is the cheapest way of being great—the easiest way of being powerful, and the happiest invention in government.... It is the most sacred thing in the constitution of America, and that which every man should be most proud and tender of. Our citizenship in the United States is our national character.... Our great title is, AMERICANS."

Chapter 5

INTERNATIONAL REVOLUTIONARY

The end of the war with England brought victory and celebration to Americans. For Paine, however, it brought an uncertain future and financial and personal woes. After the war, Paine went to stay with the Kirkbride family in Bordentown, New Jersey. These friends had housed him often in the past, and he relied on their charity again.

OPPOSITE: New York City became Paine's home in the last years of his life.

Twice he petitioned Congress to reward him for the work he had done on behalf of America during the Revolution. He detailed the services he had provided. Committees studied his case, but there were thousands of soldiers who had not yet been paid for their services, and they took priority. One committee offered to make Paine an official historian, but he turned it down. He was not interested in writing about events that had occurred—especially for a small salary. He really wanted a paid pension.

In 1784, Paine learned that Congress had no plans to honor his request for assistance. He then switched tactics and appealed to New York, Pennsylvania, and Virginia. He waited for word in Bordentown. While he battled his boredom and a painful disease called gout, he made daily trips to a local tavern. He had spent increasing amounts of time in taverns drinking over the past 5 years.

Finally, in the spring of 1785, he learned that New York had awarded him a farmhouse and more than 200 acres of land in New Rochelle, just north of Manhattan. It was presented with a citation that read, "His literary works . . . inspired the citizens of this state . . . and have ultimately contributed to the freedom, sovereignty, and independence of the United States." The next year, Pennsylvania compensated Paine with 500 pounds. In October 1785, Congress voted to award him $3,000 for his past service. (Both pounds and dollars were used as currency.) It was not as much as he had hoped for—had he taken the profits

90

from *Common Sense* alone, he would have been wealthy. Still, the awards gave Paine some financial security. He purchased a small house in New Jersey and spent his time there, in New Rochelle, and in Philadelphia.

Bridging Shores

As a craftsman, Paine had always kept an interest in mechanics. Thus, when the late 18th century brought a new age of invention, which included such innovations as James Watt's practical steam engine, Paine was eager to work with his hands again. He conducted experiments in his New Jersey home and invented a smokeless candle, which he took to Franklin, whose father had been a candle-maker. Franklin found the candles interesting, but Paine never marketed them.

By 1786, a larger project consumed his mind. As a child, Paine had lived near the town bridge in Thetford, England. As he stared at the Schuylkill River near Philadelphia, his thoughts turned to ways to bridge shores.

America's rivers had few bridges. The wooden ones that did exist had sunken pilings that were easily destroyed by ice floes in winter. Paine wanted to design a bridge made of iron that would reach from shore to shore in one span without pilings. He designed a bridge with 13 sections, one for each of the new states.

Paine hired a mechanic to help him assemble two models of the bridge. Franklin exhibited the models in his garden. A third model was made of wrought iron and displayed in the yard of the Pennsylvania State House. Paine hoped the state assembly would pay for the construction of the bridge over the Schuylkill River. The cost, however, was too high— more than $300,000 in today's money.

Franklin suggested that Paine seek investors in London and Paris to fund the project in return for a share of the tolls charged to cross the bridge. He even wrote letters of introduction for Paine. If the royal science societies in Europe supported the project, Paine might be able to encourage investors in the states, Franklin suggested.

Paine was now 50. He wanted to visit his aging parents. He also wanted to serve the government as a courier, carrying letters from American statesmen to Thomas Jefferson, the new minister in France.

Paine went first to Paris, where he arrived in May 1787. He met with Jefferson and the influential Marquis de Lafayette (Marie Joseph Paul Yves Roch Gilbert du Mortier, Marquis de Lafayette), who had served heroically under Washington in the Revolution. They introduced Paine to intellectuals and provided him with an opportunity to show his bridge design to the French Academy. No funds were offered to build it, however, because France was nearly bankrupt as a result of all the aid it had given to the Americans.

Paine sailed next across the English Channel to England. He visited his mother, who was proud of her son's accomplishments, and he also learned that his father had died almost a year before. To make his mother's later years more comfortable, Paine arranged for her to receive a small pension from the profits of his farm in New York.

In London, he pursued a patent for his bridge, and it was awarded in 1788. He had a model constructed in England, but his investor went bankrupt. Paine had hoped the bridge could be built over the River Thames in London, but that dream was

Thomas Jefferson (pictured) and Paine shared similar opinions about the nature of government.

not realized. Years later, a bridge patterned after Paine's design was built over the River Wear in Sunderland, England, although Paine did not receive any money for it.

In late 1788, when the ambassador to Great Britain, John Adams, returned to America from London, Jefferson needed someone to keep him informed of issues in England. Paine agreed to act as the unofficial minister. For the next two years, Paine traveled back and forth from London to Paris.

In 1789, French peasants stormed the Bastille to begin the bloody French Revolution.

On the Eve of Revolution

Fifteen years earlier, when Paine arrived in
America, it was on the verge of a revolution. Now,
as Paine traveled between London and Paris,
France was in the same condition. On July 14,
1789, peasants rebelled against the government
and stormed the Bastille in Paris. The old prison

was a symbol of oppression suffered by the lower classes at the hands of the king and the privileged upper class. From the Bastille, the peasants went on to attack the estates of wealthy landowners.

The ideals of the French Revolution soon spread unrest to many areas of Europe. This included England, where the Industrial Revolution had forced much of the lower class to work in dangerous and dirty factories. Many wealthy British feared that the revolution in France would provoke a similar one in Great Britain.

The Irish writer and philosopher Edmund Burke was one opponent of political upheaval. Burke, a member of Parliament, wrote a pamphlet that was critical of the French Revolution, and called it an act of "barbarism" that would cause future chaos. In his paper, he upheld the institution of monarchy, which he said deserved respect, not overthrow. He called the common people "swinish."

The upper classes in England applauded Burke's work when it was published in 1790. Commoners and thinkers such as Paine were angry. Paine had returned to England and was there when Burke's paper came out. He met with other writers who planned to write rebuttals to Burke's inflammatory and conservative paper.

Rights of Man

Soon Paine began to write a volume called *Rights of Man*. In it, he countered Burke's paper point by point and explained how democracy was superior to monarchy. When the piece was released in March 1791, it sold 50,000 copies in just a few months.

What eventually became one of Paine's most famous works argued for equality and against hereditary succession. Burke's pamphlet had defended the privilege of kings and aristocrats, and said that all people's rights are "an inheritance from our forefathers." Paine replied that he favored the "rights of the living." He called hereditary succession "an absurdity." Paine explained that the French Revolution was an attempt to remake the government into a republic. A republic was based on reason and formed with a good constitution and elected representatives. He was hopeful that the change in France could take place peacefully.

Paine went to work on a second volume of the *Rights of Man*, which he wrote in both France and England. It was published in London in February 1792, and again sold thousands of copies. In the second part, Paine again discredited monarchy and hereditary rule and called for peaceful revolution.

Paine's work claimed that good government should concern itself with the welfare of all citizens. He suggested social programs for the lower classes, such as aid to the poor, education of children, assistance for new mothers, care of the aged, and an increase in workers' wages. For the upper classes, he called for the creation of income and inheritance taxes.

Paine's work outraged the British upper class. Conservative opponents in England burned figures of Paine in effigy. The British government summoned him to appear in court. Many thought he was headed for the gallows. In September 1792, he left England for good.

★
In 1792, John Paul Jones died of kidney disease in Paris at the age of 45.
★

Revolution Gone Awry

Upon his arrival in France, Paine was hailed as a hero. In honor of his service to liberty and freedom, he was made a French citizen and elected to sit in the new National Convention. Paine's satisfaction with his honor was short-lived, because violence had erupted. In early September, radical groups had massacred more than 1,000 prisoners and soon King Louis XVI was beheaded.

While the bloodshed continued, Paine worked on a new book called *The Age of Reason*. The reigning power in France, the revolutionary party known as the Jacobins, had by this time outlawed Catholicism and Christianity and shut down the churches. This prompted Paine to question his own faith. In his new work, he wrote that he opposed organized religions.

The night he finished *The Age of Reason*, in late December 1793, he was arrested as a "foreign conspirator." The arresting officers allowed him to give his manuscript to an American friend as they led him away. *The Age of Reason* was published while he was in prison.

97

The controversial book angered many religious people, especially in America. They said Paine was an atheist, someone who does not believe in God. Paine rejected that charge and claimed that he was a deist: He believed that God was generous and good, but did not support the institution of the church.

In 1795, the head of the party that had imprisoned Paine was removed from power. A new U.S. ambassador, James Monroe, arrived in France and worked with the government to secure Paine's release in 1795, after he had been in prison for almost a year. Paine lived in Paris for the next 6 years.

Final Years

In October 1802, Paine returned to America after a 15-year absence. He was invited to visit Jefferson, now the president, in the new executive presidential mansion in Washington, D.C.

During the last years of his life, Paine wrote a number of public letters in which he explained his politics and his religious beliefs. These letters, particularly the ones in which he defended his deism, brought him new criticism. Unwelcome in many places, he moved repeatedly from his cottage in New Jersey, to Connecticut, to his farm in New Rochelle, to New York City, where he stayed with friends.

In 1805, Paine sank into a period of extreme alcohol abuse, a problem that had plagued him for the past 30 years. The next year, he suffered a stroke at age 68, and his few close friends had to care for him. In 1809, Paine made out his will, and assigned the money from the sale of his farm and land to various friends who had helped him over the years. He died on June 8, and was buried on his property in New Rochelle.

Legacy

No American statesmen came to Paine's funeral. His last years of writing had destroyed much of the respect that his early work had gained for him. In the end, Paine was a man of deeply held opinions who was able to voice them in a direct way. People who knew him well said he could be sloppy, egotistical, and annoying—especially when he drank too much. Yet Paine's contribution to the American Revolution was, in many ways, as significant as that of many people who are today considered the founders of the nation.

It has been said that the "pen is mightier than the sword," and Paine was proof of that. His writing embodied the ideals of freedom, equality, and democracy. He was devoted to revolution in order to create a government that might serve the common people, not just the privileged. He could explain his political arguments in plain terms that anyone could understand. His vision and colorful prose emboldened freedom fighters and lent hope to countless readers. The words that formed in his active mind inspired the bravest deeds of the American Revolution.

Paine's Remains

Though many people today pay homage to Paine, no one can visit his grave, because his final resting place remains a mystery. In 1819, an Englishman named William Cobbett dug up Paine's bones and shipped them to England, to memorialize the writer properly.

Somehow his remains were lost. Rumors suggest that they were misplaced in a warehouse or auctioned off for profit, or that the coffin was washed overboard in a storm at sea.

Thomas Paine's final resting place remains a mystery.

Paine himself probably would have found it most fitting that his bones should rest somewhere between two continents. He did not belong solely to one country, but devoted his life to liberty on both sides of the Atlantic. He called himself a citizen of the world.

Glossary

activism organized political action to protest policy

boycott an organized refusal to buy certain goods

confederation a union, such as the United States

Congregational a Protestant sect that governs itself

Continental Congress the first congress of united colonies

Crown the royal British monarch and government

effigy an image of a person hung or burned in protest

House of Burgesses a legislative body representing boroughs or towns in Virginia

loyalist a person who supports the ruling government

militia a body of citizens called out to fight in emergencies

Parliament the ruling legislature of Great Britain

Patriots colonists who supported and fought for their country

propaganda materials sent out by zealous members of a movement representing their views and principles

radical a person who holds extreme or contrary views

redcoats British soldiers, who wore red jacketed uniforms

repeal to withdraw officially, as a law or an act

Tory the name given to the Loyalist colonial party

treason a violation of allegiance to one's country

tyranny the abuse of power by a tyrant

zeal ardent devotion; passionate support

For More Information

Books

Coolidge, Olivia. *Tom Paine, Revolutionary.*
  New York: Charles Scribner's Sons, 1969.
Edwards, Samuel. *Rebel!: A Biography of Tom Paine.*
  New York: Praeger, 1974.
Fruchtman, Jack, Jr. *Thomas Paine: Apostle of Freedom.*
  New York: Four Walls Eight Windows, 1994.
Gurko, Leo. *Tom Paine: Freedom's Apostle.*
  New York: Thomas Y. Crowell, 1957.
Hawke, David Freeman. *Paine.* New York: Harper & Row,
  Publishers, 1974.
Kaye, Harvey J. *Thomas Paine: Firebrand of the Revolution.*
  New York: Oxford University Press, 2000.

Websites

Liberty! Chronicle of the Revolution
http://www.pbs.org/ktca/liberty/chronicle/paine.html
A brief biography with playable video and audio clips, this
page is part of a larger site on the Revolution.

Thomas Paine National Historical Association (TNPHA)
http://www.thomaspaine.org
This site has great pictures of Paine's home and memorials in
New Rochelle, as well as an archive of works and links to
writings, TPNHA events, and educational programs.

Index

Thomas Paine